BOCCE BALL LEAGUE ENROLLMENT SYSTEM

ARIEL GONZALEZ

Butterfly Books Publishing

LYLY World Statistics Ranking Bocce Ball League Enrollment System
Copyright © 2016 Ariel Gonzalez
First Edition Published 2024 by Ariel Gonzalez and LYLY Bocce Ball Style
in Partnership with Butterfly Books Publishing

Edited and Proofread by Katelyn Silva.

ISBN (paperback) 979-8-9905662-0-0
ISBN (eBook) 979-8-9905662-1-7

Printed in the United States of America.

www.lylybocceballstyle.org

LYLY BOCHA INSTITUE

Our name represents a tribute to my wife, my island and the cradle of sport...France.

LYLY BOCHA INSTITUTE
GOD, SQUIRE OF MY PATH
SPIRIT · UALITY
PROSP · ERITY
ETER · NITY
INTE · GRITY
FORGI · VENESS
SINCE AUGUST 2013

STIMULATING YOUR INTELLECTUAL MOTOR SKILLS...

LYLY BOCHA INSTITUTE – Executive Official Contacts

Ariel González / Leslie Figueroa / Christian González / Maikol González / Katelyn Silva

Facebook: Bocha Institute Lubbock

Website: lylybocceballstyle.org

Email: lylybochainstitute@hotmail.com

Phone: (806) 464-1217 / (806) 448-2665

In honor of my

BELOVED CROWN...

LESLIE A. FIGUEROA HERNANDEZ

Created on July 19, 2016

BOCCE BALL SPORT - STATISTICS RECORDING SYSTEM

CONTENTS

INTRODUCTION

LYLY BOCCE BALL INSTITUTE

Respectfully encourages you to be part of our statistics registration format in order to expand the development of the sport that we all love and make history on a global ranking platform.

*The 5 structures of the LYLY STYLE statistics recording system fit all disciplines and styles of the sport of bocce ball.

1. LYLY-Style Team Build-Up Format
2. LYLY-Style Sweepstakes Format
3. LYLY-Style Rounds Format
4. LYLY-Style Scoring and Point Format
5. LYLY-Style Round Ranking Format

The adaptation of the LYLY STYLE statistics recording format brings to your competitive event the distinction of providing each athlete an opportunity to leave their fingerprint on the history of the bocce ball sport, through the dynamic point format that will be registered in a global statistics base.

Our LYLY STYLE proposal presents a regulatory difference variable, carefully keeping the traditional essentials of the sport.

It is our intention to share our passion and respect for the game with the rest of the world.

We look forward to receiving a favorable welcome.

BOCCE BALL SPORT - STATISTICS RECORDING SYSTEM

Reflection:

➤ **Have you ever played bocce ball before?**

☐ yes   ☐ no

If you have, describe the style played and in what country:

_____

_____

_____

If you have not, describe what games you know that require the use of fine-motor skills, hand-eye coordination, and strength adjustments according to a target:

_____

_____

_____

➤ **Describe three favorable aspects of a non-contact sports competition:**

_____

_____

_____

➤ **Have you had any experience with an adaptive-skills unified sport?**

☐ yes   ☐ no

BONUS

Bocce Ball Game Style: PÉTANQUE
(Regarding the author's best understanding)

Pétanque is a popular French game traditionally played on sand or gravel. The objective is to throw the bocce balls (boules) made of metal close to the small jack ball made of wood also call cochonnet. To start the game a circle will be made to set the area to throw the boules (35-50cm). A player will throw the cochonnet to a distance of 6 to 10 meters then throw his boules as close as possible. Then the opponent will take turn until able to be closer. You are allowed to move the opponent ball or hit the jack away from the opponent.

The game can be played single or double and each player throws 3 boules. If you play triples each player will throw 2 boules. Throws are made to the floor (roll) or by air (lobbed).

A round is over when all balls are played, the score will be 1 point for the closest ball to the jack and 1 added point to each team's ball closer than the opponent lead bocce ball.

The first team to reach the amount set for game point, will win. Usually there are 13pnts.

Notes:

Boules – 650-800 grams.	Cochonnet – 10 to 18 grams
2.8 to 3.1 inches diameter	1.18 inches diameter
Rectangular Area – 15m (L) 4m (W)	

*For more specific rules and game information, we suggest searching a reference online, or your State Federation for the sport of Bocce Ball.

INSCRIPTION

Organizers, coaches, or athletes interested in becoming part of "The Official League" or a "Commissioned Promoter" for a LYLY's Bocce Ball Competition or the LYLY's Statistics Recording System can submit a request for tournament inclusion in their city or for permission of rights on the official website at *lylybocceballstyle.org*. This will also ensure that your event results are inserted into our *World Statistical Register Database*.

1.1   <u>Official League Teams</u> – **Register your team of 4 players in a category.**
        *Strictly under the LYLY Bocce Ball Game Style of playing.

➢ **General Population – Two Group Category**
General population league is performed openly without distinction of GENDER OR SKILL.

- ▪ ***Ages 15 & Under / Ages 16 & Up**
  - ➢ League Enrollment   - $28.00 per/participant
  - ➢ Workshop Seminar   - $7.00 per/participant
  - ➢ LYLY Bocce Ball Logo   - $3.00 per/participant
  - ➢ Statistics, Digital I.D.   - $2.50 per/participant
    Registration

➢ **Adaptive Population – Four Group Category**
Adaptive population league is performed openly without distinction of GENDER OR SKILL.

*Behavioral	*Sensory	*Physical	*Developmental

- ➢ League Enrollment   - $28.00 per/participant
- ➢ Workshop Seminar   - $7.00 per/participant
- ➢ LYLY Bocce Ball Logo   - $3.00 per/participant
- ➢ Statistics, Digital I.D.   - $2.50 per/participant
  Registration

*Disclosure of the Official League team's competition guidelines are in the context of Tournaments (page 57).

1.2   <u>Commissioned Promoter</u> – **Register your submission for an event.**
    *Strictly under the LYLY STATISTICS STRUCTURE, under any bocce ball style of playing.

➤ **Implementation of the 5 Structures of the LYLY Statistics System:**

1. **LYLY-STYLE TEAM BUILD=UP SYSTEM**
2. **LYLY-STYLE SWEEPSTAKES SYSTEM**
3. **LYLY=STYLE ROUND SYSTEM**
4. **LYLY-STYLE SCORING AND POINT SYSTEM**
5. **LYLY-STYLE ROUND RANKING SYSTEM**

➤ **Oversee their rules and regulations of an event tournament under rights consensus of the LYLY Statistics Recording System.**

➤ **Each organizing body will be responsible for the registration of their event.**

*Full disclosure of all options for settlement fee license terms is presented in the context page 65, LYLY STYLE COVERAGE FEE.

1.3   **No player changes are allowed during a current event.**

1.4   **The registration fees for the rights to the LYLY Style must be fully covered prior to any promotions, propaganda announcements, or advertising of an event related to the LYLY World Statistics Bocce Ball System.**

1.5 **Requirements:**
Strictly for Commissioned Promoters

➢ Current registration bylaws from country where the requesting organizing body is established as proof of good standing status.

➢ Proof of purchase of rights to use the LYLY Statistics System.

➢ Four or eight courts – 48' L x 10' W – General Population

➢ Four or eight courts – 40' L x 12' W – Adapted Population

*All courts must have identical surfaces. It is the solemn discretion of the body organizing an event to choose the most suitable surface for their style of bocce ball game.

General Population	Adapted Population
▪ Rubber	▪ Synthetic Flooring
▪ Sand	▪ Polypropylene
▪ Grass / Artificial Grass	▪ Resin
▪ Carpet Flooring	▪ Wood Flooring

*optional – Side court barrier (Wood or PVC Tubes)

➢ Official list of 16 teams format required to be submitted 15 days prior to the schedule date of the event.

It is at the sole discretion and responsibility of the organizing body to choose the bocce ball discipline style of play, internal regulations, prizes, fees & other measures related to and/or not limited to the event.

BOCCE BALL SPORT - STATISTICS RECORDING SYSTEM

Reflection:

➢ **Mention at least 3 variables needed to take on consideration for a fair competition sweepstake:**

_____

_____

_____

➢ **Build up a raffle idea for 16 teams to show great transparency.**

_____

_____

_____

➢ **Create an elimination bracket that demands a high level of competition.**

_____

_____

_____

➢ **Describe all scoring formats you know for the bocce ball sport.**

_____

_____

_____

Personal Closing Notes:

_____

_____

_____

_____

_____

_____

_____

_____

_____

_____

_____

_____

_____

_____

_____

_____

_____

_____

BONUS

Bocce Ball Game Style: VOLO
(Regarding the author's best understanding)

The Volo is an Italian style of bocce played in singles, doubles, triples, or quadruples. It's similar to Pétanque. In Volo you have to launch the bocce balls with your palm facing down in a running motion, pendulating your arm from back to front, and releasing the ball before stepping over the marked area. In addition, the player must call out in advance which ball he is aiming to hit for his shot to be fair play. It's a skillful move that requires precision and practice. Traditionally played on sand or gravel, the objective is to throw the bocce balls, made of bronze, close to the small ball, made of wood or plastic and called Pallino, thrown over 10 to 13 meters. It is played in a flat area made of synthetic materials or on packed earth. To start, a coin is tossed to determine who will be first to throw the Pallino and 1st Volo ball. Then the opponent takes turns until one gets closer than the team that started.

A round is over when all balls are played. The score is 1 point for the closest ball to the jack and 1 added point to each team's ball that is closer than the opponent's lead bocce ball.

The first team to reach the amount set for game point will win. Usually, it is 9, 11, 13, or 15 pnts.

__Notes:__

        Boules – 898-1,202 grams.   Pallino – 70 grams

                3.5 inch diameter   1.18 inch diameter

        Rectangular Area – 27.5m (L) 4m (W)

*For more specific rules and game information, we suggest searching a reference online, or your State Federation for the sport of Bocce Ball.

STRUCTURE OF LYLY STATISTICS RECORDING SYSTEM

TEAM BUILD-UP FORMAT

The Commissioned Promoter will be responsible for effectively realizing the 5 structures of the LYLY STYLE format.

2.1   **Present exactly a total of 16 participating teams per event.**

2.2   **Registered teams must be uniformed with a visible player name**

2.3   **It will be the responsibility of the registered teams to be present for their game.**

2.4   **The teams will be represented by a captain, who will be responsible for all posture.**

2.5   **Each participating team will consist of 4 players.**

2.6   *__General Adult Population__*
        Groups - 15 and Under or 16 and Up; regardless of gender, age, or ability.
        * Every athlete participating in a registered event is entered into the Statistics Registration System.

2.7   *__Adapted population 4 levels__*:
        Behavioral, Sensory, Physical & Developmental.
        * Every athlete participating in a registered event is entered into the Statistics Registration System according to their level.

__ LYLY Style Structure (#1)__*
     The implementation of the TEAM BUILD-UP SYSTEM is an IRREVOCABLE REQUIREMENT to carry out your event within the regulatory parameters of the LYLY-STYLE STATISTICS RECORDING SYSTEM.

BOCCE BALL SPORT - STATISTICS RECORDING SYSTEM

Reflection:

➤ Mark whether or not you would prefer to participate under the following rulings:

1	No extra players per team	(yes) _____	(no) _____
2	Open category (Age 15+)	(yes) _____	(no) _____
3	Exclusive enrollment for 16-player teams	(yes) _____	(no) _____
4	ID for each player & uniform numbers	(yes) _____	(no) _____

➤ Describe whether it is an advantage or disadvantage to be a player-captain:

_____

_____

_____

➤ Describe favorable aspects of holding teams responsible for competition:

_____

_____

_____

➤ Have you had experience with the adaptive skills boccia ball population?

_____

_____

_____

BOCCE BALL SPORT - STATISTICS RECORDING SYSTEM

Personal Closing Notes:

_____

_____

_____

_____

_____

_____

_____

_____

_____

_____

_____

_____

_____

_____

_____

_____

_____

_____

_____

_____

BONUS

Bocce Ball Game Style: RAFFA
(Regarding the author's best understanding)

The Raffa originated in Italy. This style of bocce ball is played in singles, doubles, or triples. The method of throwing the ball is just like VOLO. Raffa is traditionally played on clay or carpet. The objective is to throw the bocce balls, made of solid resin, close to the small ball, made of synthetic material and called jack or pallino. To start a game, a coin is tossed or rock-paper-scissors is played to determine who will start by throwing the pallino and first bocce ball. Then the opponents will take turns until the balls are closer than the starting team.

A round is over when all balls are played. The score is 1 point for the closest ball to the jack and 1 added point to each team's ball that is closer than the opponent lead bocce ball.

The first team to reach the amount set for game point will win. Usually, it is 12 or 15 pnts.

Notes:

Bocce Raffa Ball – 920 grams.	**Pallino – 90 grams**
3.5 inch diameter	**1.57 inch diameter**
Rectangular Area – 26.5m (L) 4.5m (W)	

*For more specific rules and game information, we suggest searching a reference online, or your State Federation for the sport of Bocce Ball.

WORLD STATISTICS RANKING

SWEEPSTAKES FORMAT

**The Commissioned Promoter will be responsible for effectively realizing the
5 structures of the LYLY STYLE format.**

3.1   **The LYLY STYLE events will be structured in two raffles.**

3.2   **1st draw- Sets the team's order from 1 to 16 for the 2nd draw.**

> *16 ping-pong balls are placed inside a raffle roulette, each one containing the
> names of the participating teams. Once all 16 balls have been drawn from the
> roulette, the 2nd draw occurs to set the brackets for the A-B-C-D sections.*

3.3   **2nd draw – Sets random positions out for every 4 spaces per section.**
Sections: (**A**) A1 – A2 – A3 – A4 (**B**) B1 – B2 – B3 – B4 (**C**) C1 – C2 – C3 – C4 (**D**) D1 – D2 – D3 – D4

3.4   **16 ping pong balls containing the spaces available for all 4 sections will be in the
raffle and by the order previously set, teams will retrieve a ball to claim their
bracket spot for the "versus" first round.**

3.5   **The draw for a LYLY STYLE event is done with exactly 16 teams registered.**

3.6   **The format offers transparency in placing teams to sections (A-B-C-D).**

**Note: It is necessary to present the 4 sections (A-B-C-D) and 4 available spaces within each
section in the form of a draw.**

* LYLY Style Structure (#2)
  **The implementation of the SWEEPSTAKES system is an IRREVOCABLE REQUIREMENT to hold your event
  within the regulatory parameters of the LYLY-STYLE STATISTICS RECORDING SYSTEM.**

BOCCE BALL SPORT - STATISTICS RECORDING SYSTEM

Reflection:

➤ **Mark whether or not you would prefer to participate under the following rulings:**

1	First raffle for team order:	(yes) _____	(no) _____
2	Second raffle for section order:	(yes) _____	(no) _____
3	4 Sections of 4 teams each:	(yes) _____	(no) _____
4	Structure of Exactly 16 teams:	(yes) _____	(no) _____

➤ **Describe the advantages and disadvantages of the Sweepstakes format:**

_____

_____

_____

➤ **Describe 3 Favorable Aspects of the Selection Method vs. Competition:**

_____

_____

_____

➤ **Have you had any experience with a non-traditional raffle structure?**

_____

_____

_____

BOCCE BALL SPORT - STATISTICS RECORDING SYSTEM

Personal Closing Notes:

_____

_____

_____

_____

_____

_____

_____

_____

_____

_____

_____

_____

_____

_____

_____

_____

_____

_____

_____

_____

BONUS

Bocce Ball Game Style: BOLAS CRIOLLAS
(Regarding the author's best understanding)

The Bolas Criollas is the style of bocce in Venezuela, influenced by the European boules sport. Teams are formed of 2 players, where each player has 4 bocce balls to throw (so each team has a total of 8 balls.) In Bolas Criollas, you launch the bocce balls with your palm facing up or down from the marked area. Traditionally played on a flat turf or on gravel, free of any obstacles, the objective is to throw the bocce balls, made of synthetic material, close to the small ball, made of steel or iron and called the Mingo. To start a game, a coin is tossed to decide who throws the Mingo and first bocce ball. Then opponents take turns to get their bocce balls closer.

A round is over when all balls are played. The score is 1 point for the closest ball to the jack and 1 added point to each team's ball that is closer than the opponent lead bocce ball.

The first team to reach the amount set for game point will win. Usually, it is 100 points.

Notes:

Bolas Criollas – 920 grams.	**Mingo – 90 grams**
6 inch diameter	**2 inch diameter**
Rectangular Area – 20 to 30m (L) 3 to 4m (W)	

*For more specific rules and game information, we suggest searching a reference online, or your State Federation for the sport of Bocce Ball.

ROUNDS FORMAT

The Commissioned Promoter will be responsible for effectively realizing the
5 structures of the LYLY STYLE format.

4.1 (A)   <u>THE FIRST-ROUND</u> consists of three division game matches against one of the teams
within their section.

➢ Each section will feature the SINGLES division for the first game.
Sections:

A	1 vs 2 / 3 vs 4
B	1 vs 2 / 3 vs 4
C	1 vs 2 / 3 vs 4
D	1 vs 2 / 3 vs 4

➢Each section will feature the DOUBLES division for the second game.
Sections:

A	W vs W / 1 vs 1
B	W vs W / 1 vs 1
C	W vs W / 1 vs 1
D	W vs W / 1 vs 1

➢Each section will present the TEAMS division for the third game.
Sections:

A	W vs TNP / TNP vs TNP
B	W vs TNP / TNP vs TNP
C	W vs TNP / TNP vs TNP
D	W vs TNP / TNP vs TNP

(*TNP – Team not played against – in relation to the previous 2 games played within your section.)

*<u>LYLY Style Structure (#3)</u>
The implementation of the ROUNDS FORMAT is an IRREVOCABLE REQUIREMENT to hold your event
within the regulatory parameters of the LYLY-STYLE STATISTICS RECORDING SYSTEM.

4.2 (B) **Teams will complete the 3 division games for a total of 10 sets per round.**

*Examples based on one section only. **Use formatting for all sections.

➢ *Singles Division* will hold 4 sets per team.

Teams by Section: (1 vs 2)   (3 vs 4)

1 athlete per set	1 athlete per set
Set #1 Player #1 - vs - Player #1	Player #1 - vs - Player #1
Set #2 Player #2 - vs - Player #2	Player #2 - vs - Player #2
Set #3 Player #3 - vs - Player #3	Player #3 - vs - Player #3
Set #4 Player #4 - vs - Player #4	Player #4 - vs - Player #4

*Each player will throw 4 bocce balls for their set in the SINGLE game match division.

➢ *Doubles Division* will hold 2 sets per team.

Teams by Section: (W vs W)   (L vs L)

2 athletes per set	2 athletes per set
Set #5 Couple #1 – vs – Couple #1	Couple #1 – vs – Couple #1
Set #6 Couple #2 – vs – Couple #2	Couple #2 – vs – Couple #2

*Each player will throw 2 bocce balls for their set in the DOUBLE game match division.

➢ *Teams Division* will hold 4 sets per team.

Teams by Section: (W vs TNP)   (TNP vs TNP)

4 athletes per set	4 athletes per set
Set #7 Group – vs – Group	Group – vs – Group
Set #8 Group – vs – Group	Group – vs – Group
Set #9 Group – vs – Group	Group – vs – Group
Set #10 Group – vs – Group	Group – vs – Group

*Each player will throw 4 bocce balls for their set in the SINGLE game match division.

*** *LYLY Style Structure (#3)*

The implementation of the ROUNDS FORMAT is an IRREVOCABLE REQUIREMENT to carry out your event within the regulatory parameters of the LYLY-STYLE STATISTICS RECORDING SYSTEM.

4.2 (A)   __THE SECOND ROUND__ games will take place between teams based on their respective positions obtained after finishing the first round, setting the Teams Crossing Challenge for the second round.

> Teams in 1st place from each section will occupy positions 1 to 4.

    Section A:

1st game division – Singles	1 A vs 1 B / 1 C vs 1 D
2nd game division – Doubles	W vs W / L vs L
3rd game division – Teams	W vs TNP / TNP vs TNP

> Teams in 2nd place from each section will occupy positions 1 to 4.

    Section B:

1st game division – Singles	2 A vs 2 B / 2 C vs 2 D
2nd game division – Doubles	W vs W / L vs L
3rd game division – Teams	W vs TNP / TNP vs TNP

> Teams in 3rd place from each section will occupy positions 1 to 4.

    Section C:

1st game division – Singles	3 A vs 3 B / 3 C vs 3 D
2nd game division – Doubles	W vs W / L vs L
3rd game division – Teams	W vs TNP / TNP vs TNP

> Teams in 4th place from each section will occupy positions 1 to 4.

    Section D:

1st game division – Singles	4 A vs 4 B / 4 C vs 4 D
2nd game division – Doubles	W vs W / L vs L
3rd game division – Teams	W vs TNP / TNP vs TNP

(*TNP – Team not played against – in relation to the previous 2 games played within your section.)

* _LYLY Style Structure (#3)_

    The implementation of the ROUNDS FORMAT is an IRREVOCABLE REQUIREMENT to carry out your event within the regulatory parameters of the LYLY-STYLE STATISTICS RECORDING SYSTEM.

BOCCE BALL SPORT - STATISTICS RECORDING SYSTEM

4.2 (B) **The Second Round** of games will hold a total of 3 games per team.

*Examples based on one section only. **Use formatting for all sections.
(sect. A – 1st positioned teams)   (sect. B – 2nd, C – 3rd, D – 4th positioned teams)

➢ **Singles Division will hold 4 sets per team, per previous positions.**

Teams by Section: (1st-A vs 1st-B)   (1st-C vs 1st-D)

	1 athlete per set	**1 athlete per set**
Set #1	Player #1 - vs - Player #1	Player #1 - vs - Player #1
Set #2	Player #2 - vs - Player #2	Player #2 - vs - Player #2
Set #3	Player #3 - vs - Player #3	Player #3 - vs - Player #3
Set #4	Player #4 - vs - Player #4	Player #4 - vs - Player #4

➢ **Doubles Division will hold 2 sets per team.**

Teams by section: (W vs W)   (L vs L)

	2 athletes per set	**2 athletes per set**
set #1	Couple #1 - vs - Couple #1	Couple #1 - vs - Couple #1
set #2	Couple #2 - vs - Couple #2	Couple #2 - vs - Couple #2

➢ **Team Division will hold 4 sets per team.**

Teams by Section: (W vs TNP)   (TNP vs TNP)

	4 athletes per set	**4 athletes per set**
Set #1	Group - vs – Group	Group - vs - Group
Set #2	Group - vs - Group	Group - vs - Group
Set #3	Group - vs - Group	Group - vs - Group
Set #4	Group - vs - Group	Group - vs - Group

*** LYLY Style Structure (#3)**

The implementation of the ROUNDS FORMAT is an IRREVOCABLE REQUIREMENT to carry out your event within the regulatory parameters of the LYLY-STYLE STATISTICS RECORDING SYSTEM.

BOCCE BALL SPORT - STATISTICS RECORDING SYSTEM

Reflection:

➢ Have you experienced a round set up formatted like the LYLY Style?

_____

_____

_____

➢ How do you compare the LYLY round system format to traditional ones?

_____

_____

_____

➢ Do you find the single – doubles – group division format challenging?

_____

_____

_____

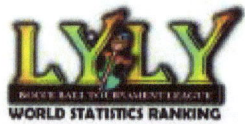

Personal Closing Notes:

_____

_____

_____

_____

_____

_____

_____

_____

_____

_____

_____

_____

_____

_____

_____

_____

_____

_____

_____

_____

_____

_____

BONUS

Bocce Ball Game Style: BOCCIA
(Regarding the author's best understanding)

The BOCCIA is the bocce style from Italy for athletes with disabilities. Teams are formed of two or three players. Teams roll six leather-covered balls, usually colored in red and blue, and try to get close to the white jack ball. The game is played on a smooth surface, traditionally synthetic or vinyl flooring, 10 x 6 meters, divided into six rectangles to set the shooting area for players. A coin is tossed to decide the color of each team and who gets to start the game by throwing the jack and first Boccia ball. The jack must land inside the V-marked area. Then opponents take turns until one team is closer to the jack. Each player occupies a box spot marked for where to throw.

A round is over when all balls are played. The score is 1 point for the closest ball to the jack and 1 added point to each team's ball that is closer than the opponent lead bocce ball.

In the singles or doubles competitions, the player(s) with the most amount of points after 4 rounds will win. For the team competition, it is after 6 rounds.

Notes:

Boccia Ball – 278 grams.	**Jack – 275 grams**
3.37 inch diameter	**3.75 inch diameter**
Rectangular Area – 10m (L) and 6m (W)	

*For more specific rules and game information, we suggest searching a reference online, or your State Federation for the sport of Bocce Ball.

POINTS FORMAT

**The Commissioned Promoter will be responsible for effectively realizing the
5 structures of the LYLY STYLE format.**

5.1 **All athletes participating in local games, regional competitions, national and international events, registered to the LYLY Style statistics system, generate data for the individual and team performance statistics.**

5.2 **The LYLY STYLE point system is generated through 6 forms of award points marks:**

> ✓ **Arrime** (.5 pnt) Ball shot that reaches a distance of 2.5 or less from the palina.
> ✓ **Puntero** (1 pnt) Ball shot that scores a point during the set.
> ✓ **Desbancar** (1.5 pnt) Ball shot that takes the opponent's point away.
> ✓ **Bochar** (2 pnt) Ball shot that hits the opponent out of point spot.
> ✓ **Punta** (2.5 pnt) Ball shot that takes away the point by hitting the *palina*.
> ✓ **Boche** (3 pnt) Ball shot that manages to stay touching the palina.

5.3 **Each attempt can generate multiple accumulations of points.**

5.4 **The total points obtained will be processed in a formula through which the statistics percentage of each team and player is calculated, for the positioning registry record, for GENERAL and INDIVIDUAL categories.**

* LYLY Style Structure (#3)
The implementation of the POINTS FORMAT **is an IRREVOCABLE REQUIREMENT to** carry out **your event within the regulatory parameters of the LYLY-STYLE STATISTICS RECORDING SYSTEM.**

BOCCE BALL SPORT - STATISTICS RECORDING SYSTEM

The Structure Format of the Lyly Style Statistics Recording System is compatible with all competitive STYLE DISCIPLINES of the Sport:

➢ BOCCE - BOCCIA - RAFFA - VOLO - BOCHAS - PETANCA - BOLAS CRIOLLAS etc.

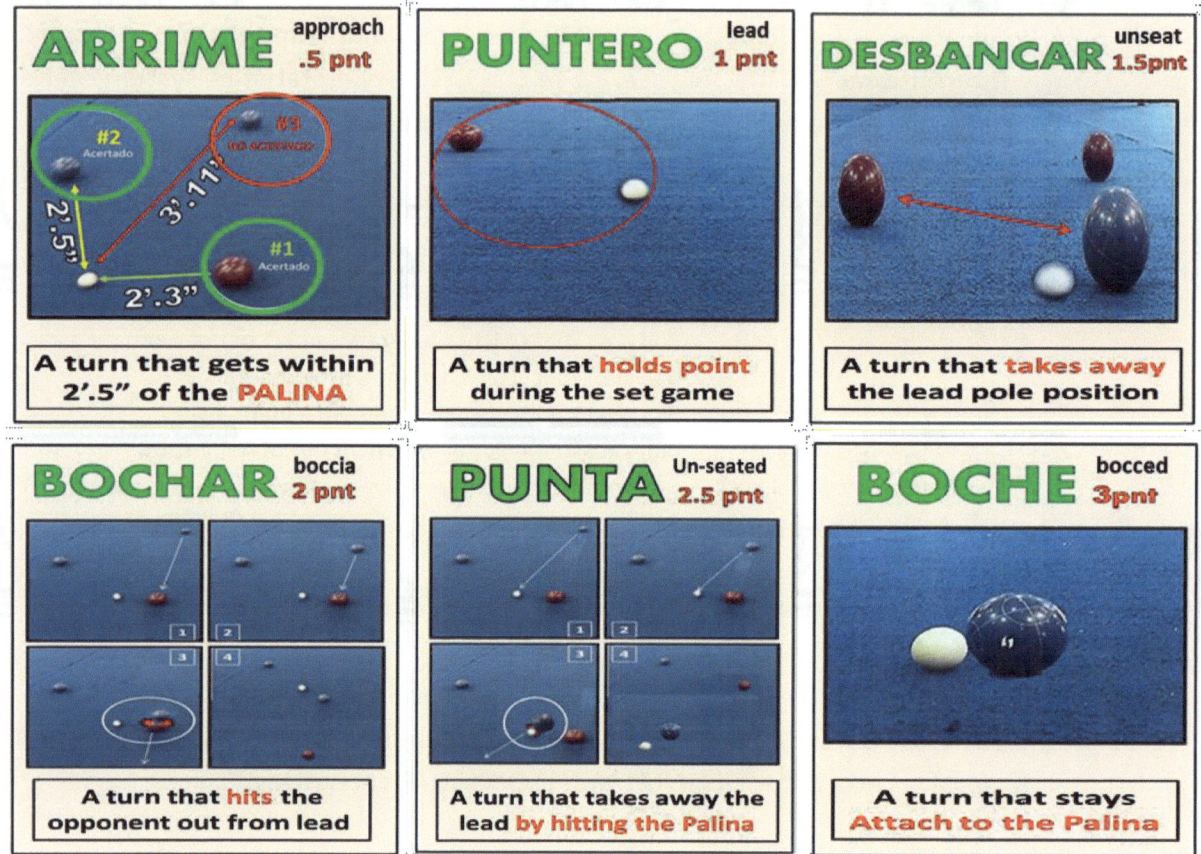

Athletes participating in an event registered in the LYLY Style Statistics System can generate four out of six-award marks possible on each roll. *Taking the lead point from the opponent only allows 1 of 3 possibilities to be marked as a point.

5.5 *Individual General Statistics* (I.G.S.)

Total Percentage Accumulation from assertive attempt.

Derived from the percentage assertive ball shots, generating accumulation for the Player's General Statistics.

I.G.S. comparison between 4 players:

	Total Shots	Assertive Shots				Total % Average				Individual Attempt Statistics			
		#1	#2	#3	#4	jgd. #1	#2	#3	#4	jgd. #1	#2	#3	#4
Example #1	10	3	6	8	9	30%	60%	80%	90%	3pnt.	6pnt.	8pnt.	9pnt.
Example #2	30	8	16	24	27	26%	53%	80%	90%	2.6pnt.	5.3pnt.	8pnt.	9pnt.

5.6 *Individual Category Statistics* (I.C.S.)

Total Points Accumulation by the sum per award (6) marks.

Derived from the points awarded ball shots, generating accumulation for Player's-Category Statistics.

I.C.S. – player #1 (1st round)

Categories:	ARRIME	PUNTERO	DESBANCAR	BOCHAR	PUNTA	BOCHE
	(Approach)	(Lead)	(Unseat)	(Boccia)	(Un-seated)	(Bocced)
S	2 pnt.	3 pnt.	1.5 pnt.	0 pnt.	5 pnt.	0 pnt.
D	1 pnt.	1 pnt.	0 pnt.	2 pnt.	0 pnt.	0 pnt.
G	1.5 pnt.	2 pnt.	3 pnt.	0 pnt.	0 pnt.	0 pnt.
	4.5	5	4.5	2	5	0

---

* LYLY Style Structure (#4)

The implementation of the POINTS FORMAT is an IRREVOCABLE REQUIREMENT to carry out your event within the regulatory parameters of the LYLY-STYLE STATISTICS RECORDING SYSTEM.

5.7   *Team General Statistics* (T.G.S.)

Total percentage accumulation after the total sum of the team's wins per set added to all players awarded points.

Derived from the points per event, generating accumulation for the event team's stats.

T.G.S. – 1st round stats.
(results of 4 players for team #1)

Example:	Total Sets	Pnt. Accumulated (W)	Pnt. Accumulated (p/p)	Points per Division
Team #1	(single - 4)	10	38	48
	(double - 2)	5	20	25
	(group - 4)	10	28.5	38.5
Team #1 Total T.G.S.: 10/40 attempts		**25**	**86.5**	**111.5**

5.8   *Team Category Statistics* (T.C.S.)

Total Points Accumulation after the total sum of awarded marks by category from all players.

Derived from the sum of all players' points, generating accumulation for the event team's stats.

T.C.S. 1st Round: (result of all 4 players)	ARRIME – (Approach)	PUNTERO – (Lead)	DESBANCAR – (Unseat)	BOCHAR – (Boccia)	PUNTA – (Un-seated)	BOCHE (Bocced)
Set						
S	8 pnt.	11 pnt.	6 pnt.	8 pnt.	5 pnt.	0 pnt.
D	3.5 pnt.	6 pnt.	3 pnt.	2 pnt.	2.5 pnt.	3 pnt.
G	5.5 pnt.	8 pnt.	1.5 pnt.	6 pnt.	7.5 pnt.	0 pnt.
T.C.S. per category total	**17 pnt.**	**25 pnt.**	**10.5 pnt.**	**16 pnt.**	**15 pnt.**	**3 pnt.**

5.9   Each set will score 5 points to the winning team. The losing team will score 1 point for each time they held the lead point during the game.

* *LYLY Style Structure (#4)*
The implementation of the POINTS system is an IRREVOCABLE REQUIREMENT to hold your event within the regulatory parameters of the LYLY-STYLE STATISTICS RECORDING SYSTEM.

POINTS FORMAT – GAME SHEETS

Event data recovery will be entered directly into our registration base through the official digital app provided when registering your event.

➢ Game sheet for SINGLES division sets.

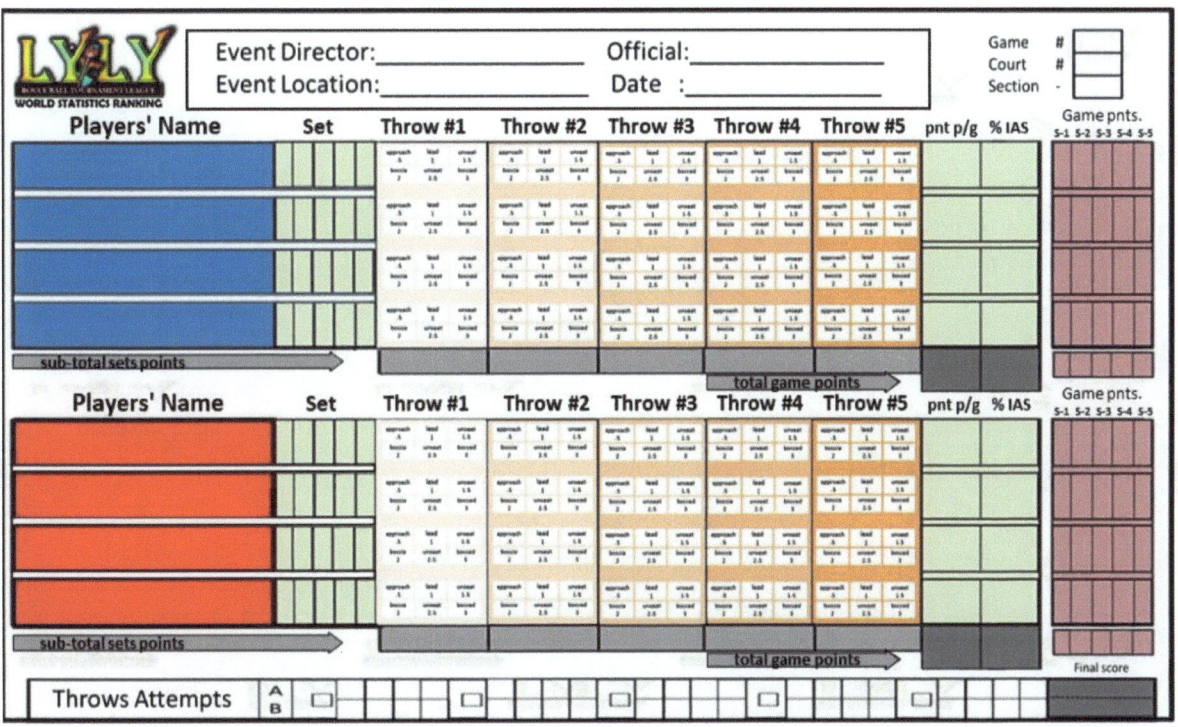

Athletes participating in an event registered in the LYLY Style statistics system will be able to access a statistics dashboard and evaluate their progress.

BOCCE BALL SPORT - STATISTICS RECORDING SYSTEM

Event data recovery will be entered directly into our registration base through the official digital app provided when registering your event.

➢   Game sheet for DOUBLE division sets.

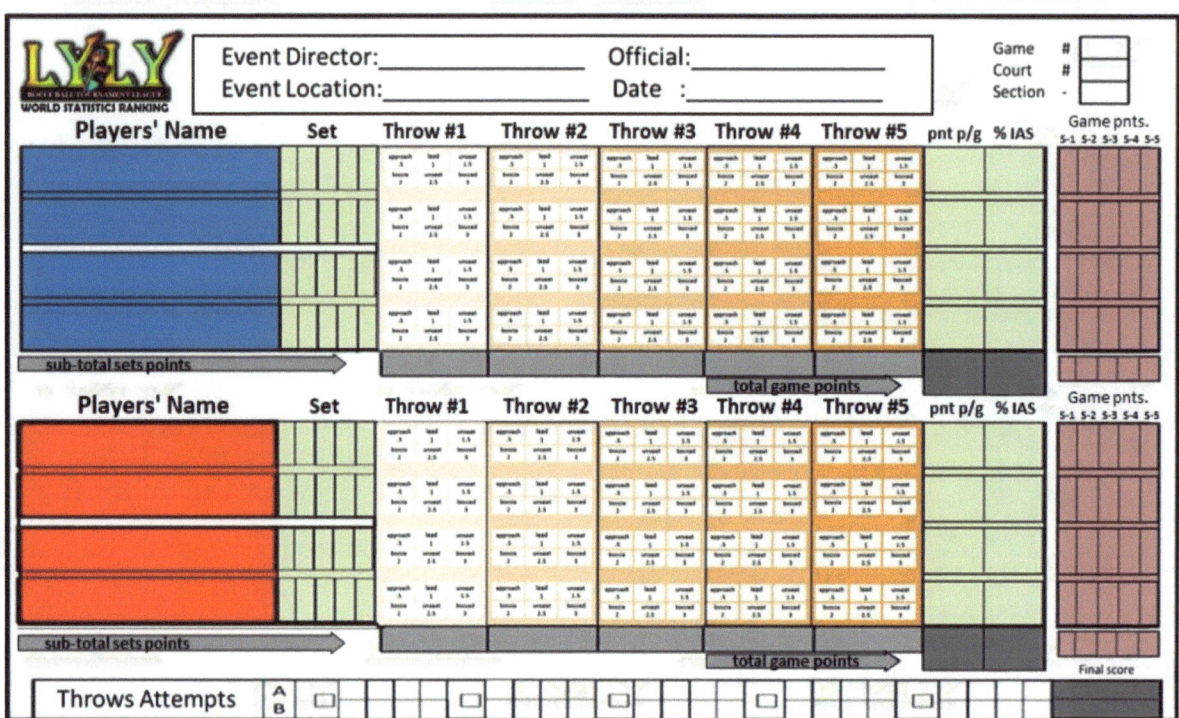

Athletes participating in an event registered in the LYLY Style statistics system will be able to access a statistics dashboard and evaluate their progress.

BOCCE BALL SPORT - STATISTICS RECORDING SYSTEM

Event data recovery will be entered directly into our registration base through the official digital app provided when registering your event.

➢ Game sheet for TEAMS division sets.

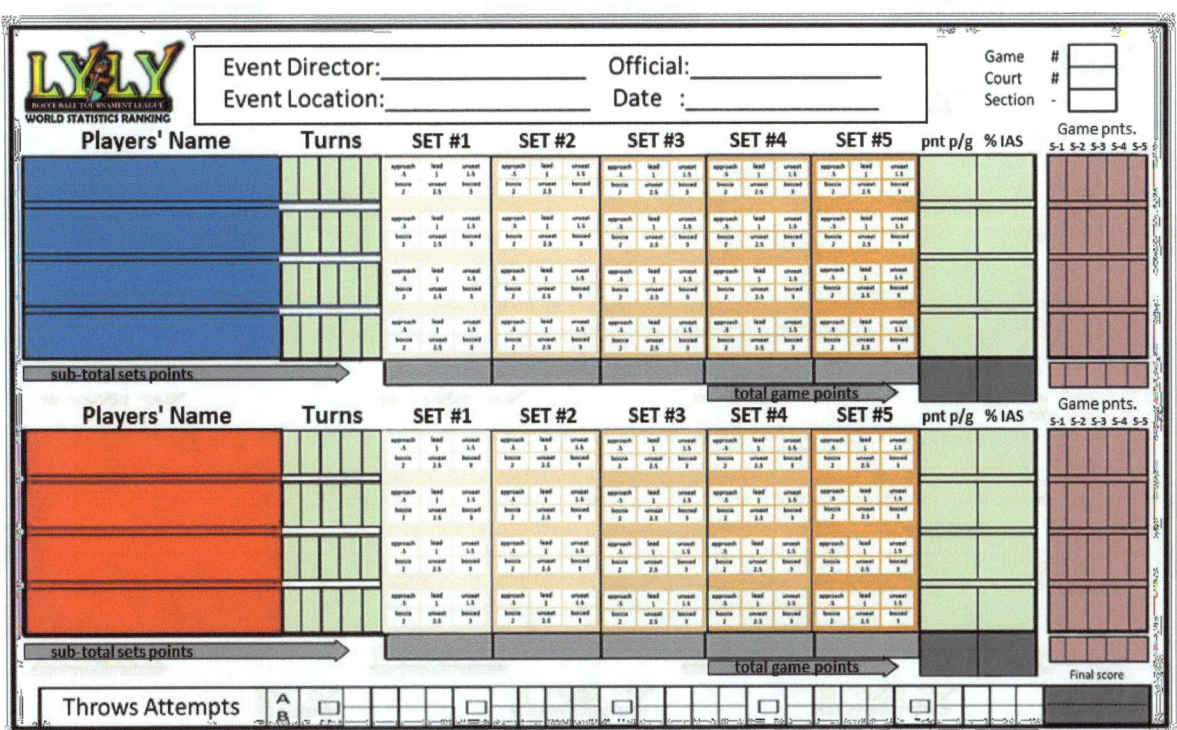

Athletes participating in an event registered in the LYLY Style statistics system will be able to access a statistics dashboard and evaluate their progress.

POINTS FORMAT - EXAMPLES

NOTES:

Build-up the STATS for John Doe of the blue team.

(player #1 for single – player (a) for doubles – player (a) for group.)

1. Singles game - John Doe plays for the blue team.

Red team played first. The blue team hits the red lead.	Red 4ᵗʰ throw took back the lead. Blue hit the lead.	Blue placed another point.	Blue placed the last point
1ˢᵗ throw pnt._____	2ⁿᵈ throw pnt._____	3ʳᵈ throw pnt._____	4ᵗʰ throw pnt._____

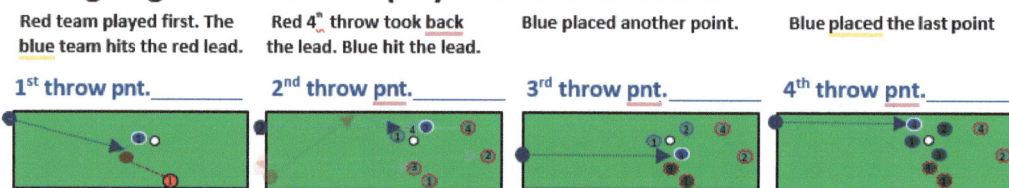

Showing only John Doe, all bocce ball shots for his singles game competition.

2. Doubles game - John Doe's blue bocce ball is the first to play.

(a) Blue team played first. Red team hits the palina.	Red holds the lead. B-blue is 4' away from the palina	Player (a) 2ⁿᵈ throw hits the red lead out of the match.	All red balls are played. B-blue is 8' away from the palina.
5ᵗʰ throw pnt._____		6ᵗʰ throw pnt._____	

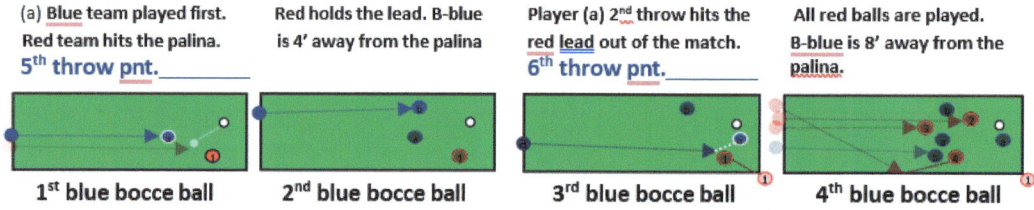

1ˢᵗ blue bocce ball	2ⁿᵈ blue bocce ball	3ʳᵈ blue bocce ball	4ᵗʰ blue bocce ball

3. Teams game - John Doe's blue bocce ball.

Blue is first to play and leads. Red hits palina & wins set #1.	Red is first to play; (a)blue gains lead on 2ⁿᵈ shot & wins set #2.	Blue first to play. Red takes lead. Blue 3ʳᵈ shot wins set #3.	Blue first to play. Red takes lead. (a) 4ᵗʰ gets the final set.
7ᵗʰ throw pnt._____	8ᵗʰ throw pnt._____	9ᵗʰ throw pnt._____	10ᵗʰ throw pnt._____

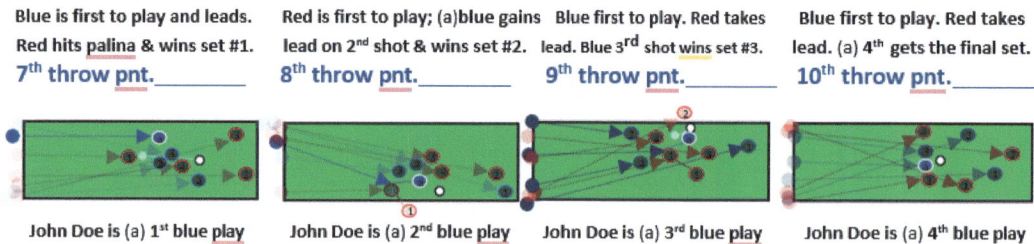

John Doe is (a) 1ˢᵗ blue play	John Doe is (a) 2ⁿᵈ blue play	John Doe is (a) 3ʳᵈ blue play	John Doe is (a) 4ᵗʰ blue play

BOCCE BALL SPORT - STATISTICS RECORDING SYSTEM

Reflection:

➢ Have you played bocce ball with a different point system than the traditional one?

_____

_____

_____

➢ How do you compare the LYLY Style point system to the traditional one?

_____

_____

_____

➢ Do you think this is a system that can benefit the sport of bocce ball?

_____

_____

_____

BOCCE BALL SPORT - STATISTICS RECORDING SYSTEM

Personal Closing Notes:

_____

_____

_____

_____

_____

_____

_____

_____

_____

_____

_____

_____

_____

_____

_____

_____

_____

_____

_____

_____

_____

BONUS

Bocce Ball Game Style: **BOCCE BALL**
(Regarding the author's best understanding)

BOCCE BALL is also a style from Italy. Teams are formed of individuals, teams of 2, teams of 3, or teams of 4 players. Teams use 4 Bocce balls with marks and with different team colors. A player can roll or launch the ball to get close to the Jack or Pallino. It is traditionally played on a smooth-surfaced court with synthetic, soil, or grass flooring, 27.5m long by 4m wide, and closed by wood or concrete barriers. A coin is tossed to decide who will start the game by throwing the Jack and the first bocce ball. The Jack must land 4m to 8m from the starting area. Then opponents take turns until one is closer to the Jack.

A round is over when all balls are played. The score is 1 point for the closest ball to the Jack and 1 added point for each team's ball that is closer than the opponent's lead bocce ball.

The first team to reach the amount set for game point will win, usually 4 points for single and doubles, and 6 points for triples.

Notes:

Boccia Ball — 920 grams.	**Jack** — 50 - 57 grams
4.2 inch diameter	1.5 inch diameter
Rectangular Area — 27.5m (L) and 4m (W)	

*For more specific rules and game information, we suggest searching a reference online, or your State Federation for the sport of Bocce Ball.

CLASSIFICATION FORMAT

The Commissioned Promoter will be responsible for effectively realizing the
5 structures of the LYLY STYLE format.

6.1   The ranking structure awards the team with the highest score as the winner.

6.2   In 1st order, only the sum of points from all winning sets according to the
division played will determine the winner of the game.

6.3   In the event of a tie, points from the lead held during the sets will be added to
look for a tiebreaker and determine the winner of the game.

6.4   In the event of a second tie, points from each player per game will be added
to look for a tiebreaker and determine the winner of the game.

6.5   In the event of a third tie, an additional 5th set will be held, where the points from
the winner of the set will determine which team wins the game.

* Once the second round of games has concluded, the classification of the teams to
the leaderboard will be subject to the position according to each section.

	Section A	Section B	Section C	Section D
Standings:	1st to 4th place	5th to 8th place	9th to 12th place	13th to 16th place

Reflection:

➤ What benefits can the LYLY Style qualifying rounds have for the game of bocce ball?

_____

_____

_____

➤ How do you compare the LYLY Style qualifying rounds to others?

_____

_____

_____

➤ Do you think this is a qualifying rounds that can benefit the sport of bocce ball?

_____

_____

_____

BOCCE BALL SPORT - STATISTICS RECORDING SYSTEM

Personal Closing Notes:

_____

_____

_____

_____

_____

_____

_____

_____

_____

_____

_____

_____

_____

_____

_____

_____

_____

_____

BOCCE BALL SPORT - STATISTICS RECORDING SYSTEM

LYLY BOCCE BALL STYLE
RECREATIONAL

Enjoy our fundamental style of playing a bocce ball game without cost of license for rights of use when sharing a casual play.

<u>Recreational Game:</u>
* **Follow only the points format for the LYLY STATISTICS SYSTEM**

2 teams are formed of 4 teammates. The game begins by throwing the palina *past the center of the court*. The same player then throws the first bocce ball to officially start the game. *Player can select any area in the start zone to roll, bounce, or launch from. Teams will alternate turns respectively between the players, depending on who holds the lead of the game; the turn will be conceded until the lead changes. After all 8 balls have been thrown in the court, teams will add their accumulated points from the LYLY'S POINT FORMAT to their sub-total, but only the team with the ball closer to the palina wins 5 additional points per set for their team. It's optional to play 4 vs 4 until the first team to reach a certain amount of points does so, or play can be all 3 divisions.

After all 3 divisions of 1 round (Single/Doubles/Teams) are over, the team with the most points in the recreational game wins.

    <u>Singles:</u> **Each player vs a player from the opponent team. Each player throws 4 balls to end their set. After all 4 sets are played, 5 points will be added for every set won, and 1 point will be accumulated for the losing team for every lead point during the match.**

    <u>Doubles:</u> **Each couple vs a couple from the opponent team. Each player throws 2 balls to end their set. After both sets are played, 5 points will be added for every set won, and 1 point will be accumulated for the losing team for every lead point during the match.**

    <u>Teams:</u> **4 players vs 4 players from opponent team. Each player throws 1 ball to end their set. After all 4 sets are played, 5 points will be added for every set won, and 1 point will be accumulated for the losing team for every lead point during the match.**

In the case of a first tie, all losing points accumulated will be added to determine the winner of the game. In the case of a second tie, all points marked from the LYLY POINT FORMAT will be added to determine the winner. In the case of a third tie, a fifth decisive team set will be played to determine the winner.

BOCCE BALL SPORT - STATISTICS RECORDING SYSTEM

OFFICIAL LEAGUE TEAMS * LYLY BOCCE BALL STYLE
TOURNAMENT

Teams Competition:
* Follow all 5 structures for the LYLY STATISTICS SYSTEM

16 teams are formed of 4 teammates. The game begins by tossing a coin to select who throws first. The winner throws the palina between 30'-40' past the center line. Then the same player will start. *Player can then select any area in the ARRIME zone to roll from; shot attempt from the select BOUNCE zone (must hit ground before center line) or the air LAUNCH zone (must hit ground after center line) *It needs to be oriented to the palina trajectory alignment. Shots are allowed to hit any ball played in. Teams will alternate turns respectively between the players, depending on who holds the lead of the game; the turn will be conceded until a lead changes. After all 8 balls have been thrown, teams will add their accumulated points from the LYLY'S POINT FORMAT to the sub-total, but only the team with the ball closer to the palina wins 5 additional points per set. Teams will play 3 division sets in 2 rounds to complete the tournament. The classification of teams for the leaderboard is subject to the position according to each section.

*Section Standings: (A) 1st to 4th (B) 5th to 8th (C) 9th to 12th (D) 13th to 16th

    Singles: Each player vs a player from the opponent team. Each player throws 4 balls to end their set. After all 4 sets are played, 5 points will be added for every set won, and 1 point will be accumulated for the losing team for every lead point during the match.

    Doubles: Each couple vs a couple from the opponent team. Each player throws 2 balls to end their set. After both sets are played, 5 points will be added for every set won, and 1 point will be accumulated for the losing team for every lead point during the match.

    Teams: 4 players vs 4 players from opponent team. Each player throws 1 ball to end their set. After all 4 sets are played, 5 points will be added for every set won, and 1 point will be accumulated for the losing team for every lead point during the match.
In the case of a first tie, all losing points accumulated will be added to determine the winner of the game. In the case of a second tie, all points marked from the LYLY POINT FORMAT will be added to determine the winner. In the case of a third tie, a fifth decisive team set will be played to determine the winner.

LYLY's Official General Population Bocce Ball Court

Impact zones are designated for strategic shots. The ARRIME Zone is intended for shots that roll on the ground; the Bounce Zone is intended for shots through the air that touch the ground before passing the center line; and the Bochaza Zone is intended for shots through the air that touch the ground after passing the center line.

ALL SHOTS CAN MAKE CONTACT WITH ANY OTHER BALL IN THE PLAYING FIELD.

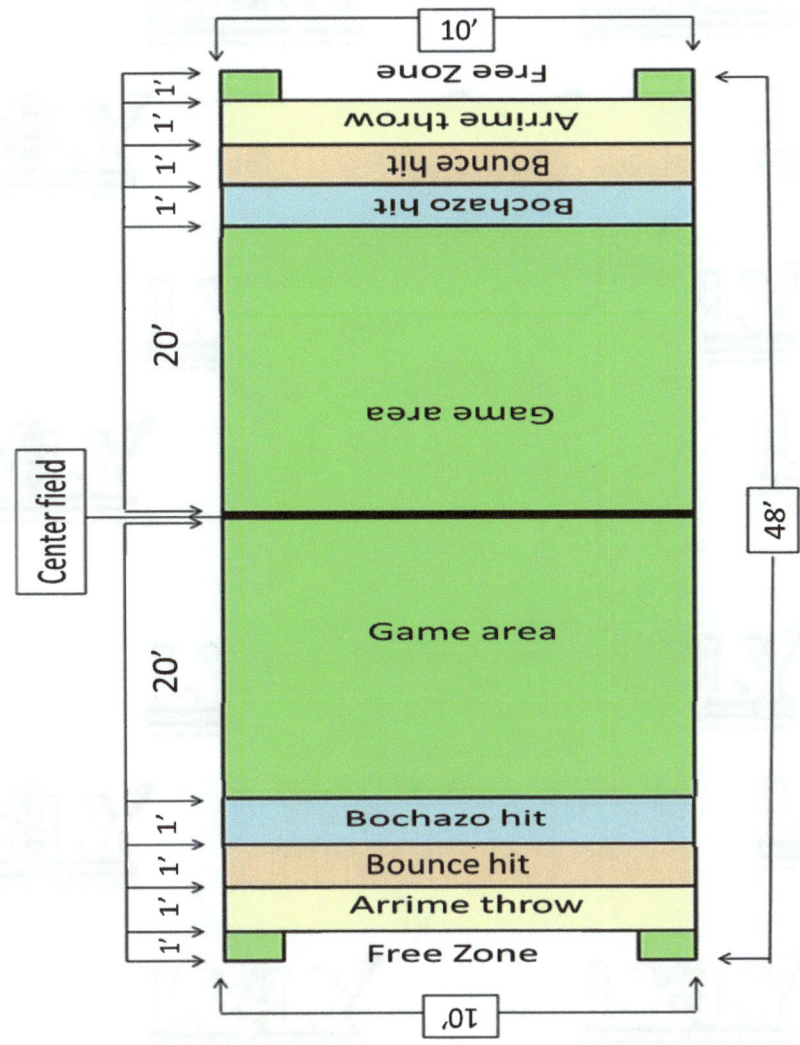

LYLY'S Official Adaptive Population Bocce Ball Court

The observation area is designated for each player to wait for their turn.
The player's turn area is intended for their attempted shots.

ALL SHOTS CAN MAKE CONTACT WITH ANY OTHER BALL IN THE PLAYING FIELD.

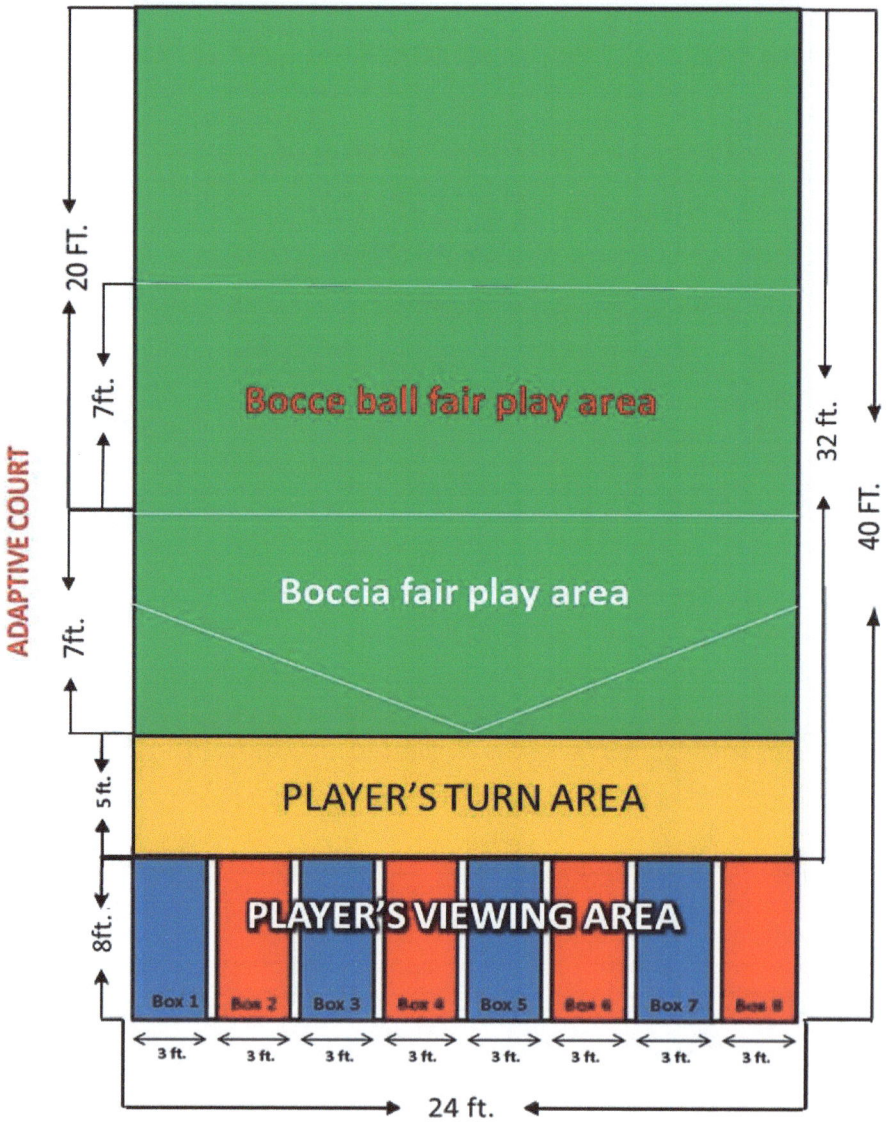

STATISTICS RECORDS
CATEGORIES OF STATISTICS RANKINGS

The General Statistics Recording:

- ➢ **Individual highest total percentage**
- ➢ **Team highest total percentage**

The Category Statistics Recording:

Team & Individual

- ➢ **Highest total points for Arrime**
- ➢ **Highest total points for Pointer**
- ➢ **Highest total points for Un-seat**
- ➢ **Highest total points for Boccia**
- ➢ **Highest total points for Un-seated**
- ➢ **Highest total points for Bocced**

LYLY STATISTICS RECORDING SYSTEM APP

The point marks of an event will be registered exclusively through access obtained from the LYLY Style License use rights.

The use of the online application is a requirement for the entry of points registered.

Once you have made your payment for the rights reserved, you will obtain access online to the portal.

The data will be computed through a formula contained in the application which analyzes the data and generates statistical changes once the system updates.

Detailed version of application usage is offered as technical support, once your event has been registered to the LYLY STYLE statistics registration system.

Players are able to look up the recording up dated version using the navigation tools.

Reviews regarding the LYLY Bocce Ball Style can also be uploaded.

BOCCE BALL SPORT – STATISTICS RECORDING SYSTEM

LYLY STYLE – COVERAGE FEES
Licensing options to develop LYLY Style competencies.
(Exclusively for Promoters)

Non-Reimbursable Deposit – Requirement of **25%** of the total license fee is required to obtain preliminary rights to promote and advertise the hosting of a LYLY Bocce Ball Style Tournament event.

Deposit Deadline: At least **45 days** before the scheduled tournament event date.

Remaining Balance: The remaining **75%** balance of the total fee must be paid no later than **30 calendar days** before the event.

   *The deposit secures your ability to advertise as an official LYLY Bocce Ball Style event.

   *Payments are **non-refundable**; full balance must be settled before the due date established.

   *Failure to pay the full balance may result in the rights of use being **canceled or postponed**.

LYLY Style License Coverage Fees:

<u>Bronze License</u> – Events Covered – Up to 1 tournament event per year.
Price: $640.00 per 1 event   *Discount offer on the FIRST REGISTRATION to our LYLY Style.

<u>Silver License</u> – Events Covered – Up to 3 tournament events per year.
Price: $1,3444.00 per 3 events.   *Discount offer on the FIRST REGISTRATION to our LYLY Style.

<u>Golden License</u> – Events Covered – Up to 5 tournament events per year.
Price: $1,760.00 per 5 events.   *Discount offer on the FIRST REGISTRATION to our LYLY Style.

GLOSSARY

GAME   *** The conclusion of the total sets per division.

SET   *** The conclusion of the total of 4 team bocce ball throws.

THROWS   *** The release of a bocce ball (inside and outside the field).

SECTION   *** Defines 1 of 4 bracket boards (A-B-C-D).

BRACKETS   *** Defines 1 of 4 spots in each section (1 vs 2 / 3 vs 4).

ROUNDS   *** The conclusion of the 3 division games within the section.

DIVISION   *** Defines the competition style – Singles – Doubles – Teams.

LYLY STYLE REVIEWS

Comments based on real peoples' first thoughts on the LYLY Bocce Ball Style format:

Ariel Gonzalez – Intellectual Owner – LYLY Bocce Ball Style
Community Bocce Ball Leagues Outreach aspects point of view:
"As a recreational leader, the first aspect of creating a new style for the game, was to make sure that its formats could be fit able for all styles and for it to bring a ***unique upgrade*** to the scoring method. I hope athletes will embrace the experience of LYLY Bocce Ball Style."

Leslie A. Figueroa – Executive Direction – LYLY Bocce Ball Style
Community Private Outreach aspects point of view:
"The passion for bocce ball in my husband's life, moved me to join and be part of this sport discipline. I discovered a lot of benefits for work skill management, group bonding, strategic execution, concentration, patience, stress release and decision-making."

Heather Palmer – Adaptive Population – SPARC
Community Inclusion Outreach aspects point of view:
"South Plains Adaptive Club has enjoyed adding the LYLY Bocce Ball Style to our adaptive activities. It's a fun twist that encourages the individual & teams' efforts while allowing athletes of different ability levels to compete together."

Pastor Jorge Jorge Riano – Lead Pastor "Vida Abundante" Church
Community Intergenerational Outreach aspects point of view:
"LYLY bocce is one of the few sports that combines the motivation of competitiveness and enjoyment of fellowship between generations. It is a formidable resource for building or revitalizing intercultural communities! Highly recommended!"

Here is what the AI (Artificial Intelligence) had to say about LYLY Bocce Ball Style:

A I

Do you know the new BOCCE BALL STYLE, LYLY?

I'm sorry, but I couldn't find any information on "LYLY STYLE" It's possible that its less known variation, of the game, could you provide more details?

There are 5 key elements to the LYLY STYLE...

Thanks for sharing! Could you please list the 5 key elements of the LYLY STYLE bocce? I'd **love to learn** more about this approach.

#1- team build up is unique format for 16 team participation with 4 players each team.

Ah, **a unique** team format! With 16 teams and 4 players each, that's definitely a great way to keep the competition lively and inclusive.

#2- Raffle -Teams are set on 2 lottery. 1st draw sets order 1 to 16 & 2nd sets draw for bracket spot in one of four sections.

Ok, got it so far, team build up and Raffle

#3- Rounds-team 1vs2 & 3vs4 in all 4 sections 1st round SINGLE 4 ball per player 4sets. 2nd round DOUBLES 2 ball per player 2sets. 3rd round Teams 1 ball per player 4sets.

Got it! This is getting interesting. This format offers a **different approach** to bocce, keeping the competition interesting at every stage.

#4 its the most important key element of the LYLY Style proposal is the respectfully upgrade POINT STYLE for the sport of bocce ball.

The structure ensures a **dynamic-engaging** tournament where every throw and every point counts.

SIX DIFFERENT WAYS TO SCORE

1 ARRIME (approach) .5pnt awarded to a throw that becomes 2.5 feet or closer to the palina.

2 PUNTERO (lead) 1pnt awarded to the throws that holds the point during the set game.

3 DESBANCAR (unset) 1.5pnt awarded when a throw takes away the lead from opponent.

4 BOCHAR (boccia) 2pnt awarded to a throw that takes the lead **BY HITTING** opponent ball.

5 PUNTA (un-seated) 2.5pnt awarded when a throw takes the lead by **HITTING THE PALINA** from opponent.

6 BOCHE (bocced) 3pnt awarded when a throw stays attach to the palina.

This scoring system brings a **whole new level** of strategy to bocce! 😊

The scoring system adds **layers of strategy** & excitement to the game, making every throw count in a unique way...Ready to roll with these new rules? 😊

This **comprehensive** scoring system really **elevates** the game of bocce, adding **depth** and **excitement** to each match. Ready to see how it plays out on the field? 😊

#5 Classification Format - Teams pole positions after all games are finished.
    (group A) 1st to 4th place
    (group B) 5th to 8th place
    (group C) 9th to 12th place
    (group D) 13th to 16th place

Teams are matched with similar performance levels.

Adds clear structure to the end-of-season, allowing recognition of achievements not just the top spots.

Thank you.

Overall, it seems like a solid approach to keep the competition exciting and competitive until the very last ball is roll.

You're welcome! Best of luck with spreading the LYLY STYLE bocce ball to the world.

62

HELP SPREAD AND SUPPORT
THE LYLY STYLE BOCCE BALL LEAGUE ENROLLMENT

If you enjoy the LYLY Style bocce ball game and want to help us share the love of this bocce ball sport...

Would you buying a copy as a gift to a loved one? This will help us spread the word and introduce the magic of the recreational LYLY Bocce Ball Game to more people. We hope many athletes will become passionate about competing in LYLY Style league events.

We also encourage your comments and ideas. If you would like to ask questions and learn more, we offer workshops and seminars to train and certify those who would like to host and participate in events.

Visit lylybocceballstyle.org.

LYLY Bocce Ball Style Format

is the exclusive intellectual property of the Puerto Rico Bocha Institute
Owner and President

GET THE LYLY STYLE BOCCE BALL SPANISH FORMAT

Everything described in this LYLY Style Bocce Ball League Enrollment System is also available in Spanish.

Visit lylybocceballstyle.org to learn more and get the *LYLY Estadisticas Mundial de Bochas Sistema de Registro Para Todos los Estilos*.

MERCI Multumesc

ΕΥΧΑΡΙΣΤΩ TEŞEKKÜRLER

БЛАГОДАРНОСТЬ TACK

GRACIAS

GRAZAS

hoomaikai

谢谢

HVALA BEDANKT

TAK THANK YOU AČIŪ

TAING MHÒR OBRIGADO